ELIJAH
THE
WICKED QUEEN

I Kings 19—II Kings 9 FOR CHILDREN

Written by Louise Ulmer
Illustrated by Jim Roberts

COPYRIGHT © 1976 CONCORDIA PUBLISHING HOUSE, ST. LOUIS, MISSOURI

MANUFACTURED IN THE UNITED STATES OF AMERICA

ALL RIGHTS RESERVED

ISBN 0-570-06101-6

Publishing House
St. Louis

ARCH Books

A little girl named Stephanie
Worked very hard and carefully
Sewing for great Queen Jezebel,
The wickedest queen of all.

When Jezebel sang, "I'm so lovely and rich!"
Stephanie thought she looked more like a witch,
With her eyelids painted purple and green
And her cheeks the reddest you've ever seen.

Well, the thing that bothered Jezebel
Was the God her people loved so well.
"Your God is old fashioned," she said with
a smile.
"I'll bring in my own and we'll try them
awhile."

"I'm tired of goodness and kindness and such!
You'll like my gods better, I promise as much."
So she had some new temples built, fancy and
      high,
For gods of the weather, the rivers, the sky.

When Stephanie asked, "What can these gods
      do?
What's wrong with our God, who is real and
      true?"
Jezebel said, "I want gods I can see,
Like Baal, who is god of the plant and the
      tree."

King Ahab was Jezebel's husband's name.
The way she bossed him was really a shame.
But Elijah the preacher, Jezebel found,
Was a man of God she could not push around.

For Elijah was sent by the Lord to say,
"Those silly clay gods must be taken away.
They're nothing but dolls, so get rid of them
    now.
Tear down those statues and that golden cow!

"The God that I worship rules earth and sky.
You cannot replace Him, however you try.
And you will be gentle and good and true,
If Jehovah, the Lord, is your God too."

"That preacher Elijah is just an old fool.
He tells me I'm selfish and hateful and cruel,"
Said Jezebel. "No one talks back to me!
I'll fix that man yet, just you wait and see."

When Ahab wanted a grape farm one day,
He went to the farmer and offered to pay.
"This is mighty fine land here, my friend,
    mighty nice.
If you sell it to me, I'll pay a fine price."

"I'm sorry, your majesty," Naboth replied,
"But this farm that you want is my joy and
    my pride."
When Naboth the farmer refused to sell out,
King Ahab went home to his bedroom to pout.

But Stephanie heard of the awful crime;
She went for Elijah who came in no time.
Elijah was mad when he saw the king's face.
"What gives you the right to take over this
　　place?

"While you were home pouting in bed today,
Your wife killed a man since he got in her
way.
She does as she pleases and you don't care.
No one can stop her for nobody dares.

"So I have a warning for her from the Lord.
You take her this message and give her the
    word.
Jezebel thinks she is clever and rich,
But the Lord knows her heart is the heart of
    a witch."

Then Ahab was scared for his very life.
He feared the Lord even more than his wife.
"And you're not much better, King Ahab, my
    friend.
The days of your meanness must come to an
    end."

When the warning was given as plain as
    could be,
Said Jezebel, furious, "You can't scare me!
I'm queen of this land and no one can top me.
I'll do as I please and no one can stop me!"

The warning from God seemed to do her no
   good.
She did as she pleased, like she said she
   would.
"I'll show that Elijah and Ahab too,
That my gods are better. That's just what I'll
   do."

But people grew tired of her lies and schemes.
And some of them hated the gods of the queen.
So a new king was chosen in Israel,
And they kept it a secret from Jezebel.

When at last she heard that the new king
was near,
Was Jezebel worried and filled with fear?
She said, "He can't hurt me; he wouldn't
dare!
Baal will protect me. I'll go fix my hair."

When the good king's army marched into
town,
From a high palace window the queen looked
down.
Three servants behind her were watching the
scene.
They gave her a push and she fell with
a scream.

And that was the end of Jezebel
And the silly clay gods she liked so well.
She might have been pretty, and clever, and
   rich,
But the Lord knew her heart was the heart of
   a witch.

So the people and little Stephanie
Were free from Baal, the god of the tree,
Were free to worship the Lord above,
The God of goodness and kindness and love.

DEAR PARENTS:

This story is really one of contrast between two children: the willful, petulant child Jezebel, who was queen, and the sensitive, responsible child Stephanie. It is also a contrast between two gods: the play god Baal, who is god of things (trees, rivers, etc.), and our God, Jehovah, who is God of people.

To make sure your child sees how childish Jezebel actually was, it might pay to check back through the story and pinpoint some of the characterizing details and language, e. g., she gets tired of things, so she changes them; her gods are "dolls"; she gets the vineyard for her childish husband; she says, "You can't scare me," etc.

Notice also how she treats everything as her toy. Yet, throughout the story sounds the refrain, "Her heart is the heart of a witch." Her world view is really very pessimistic. And her not caring about anyone but herself transforms her world into an ugly thing where a man can be killed on a whim.

This story gives you the opportunity as Christian parents to help your children distinguish between what is real and what is fantasy. Explore with them the differences between toys and people (between make-believe and reality). Gently introduce them to the idea of joyful seriousness — that is, of treating all creation with respect and love because we all are made precious through Christ's death and resurrection. And let them know that they are loving and lovable because God has created in them beautiful hearts.

THE EDITOR